Fear Emporium

Magpie The Poet

BookLeaf Publishing

India | USA | UK

Presentation by *BookLeaf Publishing*

Web: www.bookleafpub.com

E-mail: info@bookleafpub.com

ISBN: 978-93-5744-340-1

First edition 2022

The Curious "Shop"

Admiring the beach front stores, I noticed
A quaint and quiet shop. A tourist trap.
"Fear Emporium" the sign said, focused
It was watching, its stare would make me snap.
A sturdy wooden door keeping us out
But an open sign beckoning us in
My internal conflict, I had some doubt
What's inside? I need to know what's within . . .
Firmly, I gripped the door handle, unsure
Unexpectedly, it opened simply
Thought a place like this would be more secure
Inside it was met dimly, grimly.
Strange artefacts lined the walls, floor and more
I guess all there is to do now is explore.

Arachnophobia

The first exhibit to catch my eye,
A glass terrarium, octagonal and full
Succulents surrounding small stones
A circular clearing in the centre

Dancing above the clearing,
A net of steel silk
Corpses littering the web
Like lights on Christmas.

Previously unseen, the brute
Slowly, agonizingly it crawls
It creeps
It stares
And, suddenly
It leaps.

Pounding down upon a poor unsuspecting,
Powerless victim
There was no scream nor cry
There was no resistance
There was only accepting fate
They will die

Goodbye Mr Spider.

Ophidiophobia

Sat sulking suddenly
A basket
Stood side by side
An instrument

"Ophidiophobia
Fear of Snakes
Lift the lid
At your own risk"

"Charm the snake
Otherwise, you'll
Seal your fate"

The basket shuddered
Shook, sibilated
I turned away.
Let the snake lie.

Equinophobia

Hung on a bare patch of wall
A split horseshoe
From the second place horse
Unlucky it split
The strength
The speed
To snap iron clean
I wouldn't want to be underneath

Coulrophobia

There once was a happy clown
He travelled from town to town
The children would cry
Whenever he came by
So now he's trapped with a frown

Claustrophobia

A spacious glass jar
A metal lid with no holes
A person stood in the centre

The tag below read
"Claustrophobia, fear of confined spaces
rotate the jar"

Suddenly, a cramped glass prison
A metal lid sealing fate
A person taking up such little space.

Thalassophobia

In the floor,
A window
To the depths,
Below

The endless, eternal
Sinking
Losing energy,
Drowning

People falling
Continuously
Some are just specks.
Surprisingly

The creatures swimming
Know
They watch the life
Go
Their paralysis is "thalassophobia"

Trypophobia

A specimen box, locked
"Trypophobia
A common fear found in people
The small holes scare then"

Each compartment contained something new
Beeswax, sea sponges, strawberry seeds.
Lotus flower, concrete bubbles, bread's holes,
Coral, pomegranates, eye clusters.

And in each and every hole
A figure trying to escape
But they can't get away

Trypanophobia

"Trypanophobia, fear of needles"
"A small collection"
They circle a figure
Each with their own use

The healing jab of the medicinal syringe
The slow drag of the tattoo pen
The positive stab of filiform needles
The mending pull of sewing pins

All terrify the surrounded person
Scratching under their skin.

Hemophobia

Standing in the corner, a single bag
Catheter circling through the holder
"Hemophobia" it said on the tag
Held by metal, making the room colder
A constant cycle of deep crimson red
In the centre, a terrified person.
You can see it in their eyes; the pure dread.
Thrashing will only make their case worsen
Drowning in the thick scarlet solution
The stench of iron seeped into their mind
"So unclean! Id prefer execution."
The drip of blood, their fate. So intertwined.
Drip... drip... drip... the cycle will continue...
They see the flow outside and within you.

The Door

On the back wall there was a sturdy door
I had a deeper curiosity
Certainly more now than ever before
My new knowledge woke a ferocity
A sign told me. "Enter at your own risk"
"We are not responsible for damage"
"Mental or phy-" Oh just get on with this!
I didn't read the rest. I was savage
This room was dimmer. It wasn't as full.
There were still objects, but the air's changed
I felt a sense of dread, but I am pulled
By these artefacts, peculiar and strange
"Intangible" was carved into the floor
Have I been to greedy Asking for more?

Glossophobia

A podium tarried, tuckered into the corner.
Ominous in the hazy light
Sharp, angular edges, never worn in.
"Glossophobia, fear of public speaking"

On top of the shelf
Garbled notes with a microphone
Matchstick figures in a circle
Standing neutrally, intimidatingly

In the heart of the crowd
One individual, paranoid to disappoint
Too many people, too many words
They can't take it anymore

Deafening Silence.

Xenophobia

Fear of the unknown
A darkened box, on its own
What's inside? A stone?
A bone? A phone?
A don't know
What lies outside our zone?
When can we know?
What do we have to outgrow?
Who do we have to overthrow?
To see the contents of that box on its own
Xenophobia, fear of the unknown

Atychiphobia

On the bottom shelf
A shoebox diorama
Half-smashed, carved in.
An empty classroom.

Save for a lone child
Hunched over their paper test
Back turned, face down.
A hard worker.

As the light swung in their favour
It illuminated their failing test papers
And just for a moment,
You could feel yourself in their shoes.

The "F"s, the "D"s
The three marks away from passing
So close, yet so far
The anxiety of failing again.

Scoptophobia

15

On the ceiling, Scoptophobia
The Eye of Providence, all seeing
Nowhere to hide
Not an issue if you have nothing to hide
Nowhere to hide
The firm gaze on your back
Nowhere to hide
The terror sets in
How long has it been watching?
Scoptophobia

Autophobia

One matchstick person
In a matchstick box
Polaroid photos,
Friends or foes?
It doesn't matter now
They are alone

Alone is chose
Four grey walls.
Portals to the past.
Memoirs of before.
Colour lost
Bleeding onto the floor.

One grey person
In a grey box
Monochrome photos
Dripping colour
Dripping life
They are still alone...

Philophobia

17

Philophobia, it's the fear of love
A returned red velvet box sat alone
No words needed, there's nothing to speak of
It didn't work, the reason is unknown
Diamonds should be forever, that is true
One is scared, the other is asking 'why?'
Two broken hearts, the fear split them in two
This box was returned after their goodbye

Athazagoraphobia

In a crowed room
With busy people
You watch calmly
As one steps up
To the centre
It asks.
"How many remember?"

One by one
The people leave
Friends, family, total strangers
They must've just been
A face in the crowd
They've lost everyone
Completely forgotten.

Gerascophobia

On the middle shelf of the cabinet
There was an hourglass
The fine golden
Sand was
Running
Down
Dow
N
Down
Onto an
Unsuspecting
Figure in the bottom
Half, you can see them
Age, and not long is left

Thanatophobia

This was the final one.
A mahogany casket.
But, who was inside...?

The Tourist Trap

Amongst the other beach front stores, we stood
A cruel and cacophonous tourist trap.
"Fear Emporium" now I understood
I was watching, waiting for them to snap
A sturdy wooden door keeping us in
Even so, could we also keep them out?
We didn't want the vile building to win
"Stop being curious" we tried to shout.
We hoped they were leaving, they seem unsure
They were hesitating, just turn around
Yet their interest won, they opened the door . . .
We've seen it before, we know what they found
The alluring exhibits wall to wall
And what's behind that door, we've seen it all . . .